How to Invest for Young Investors by a Young Investor

Jack Rosenthal

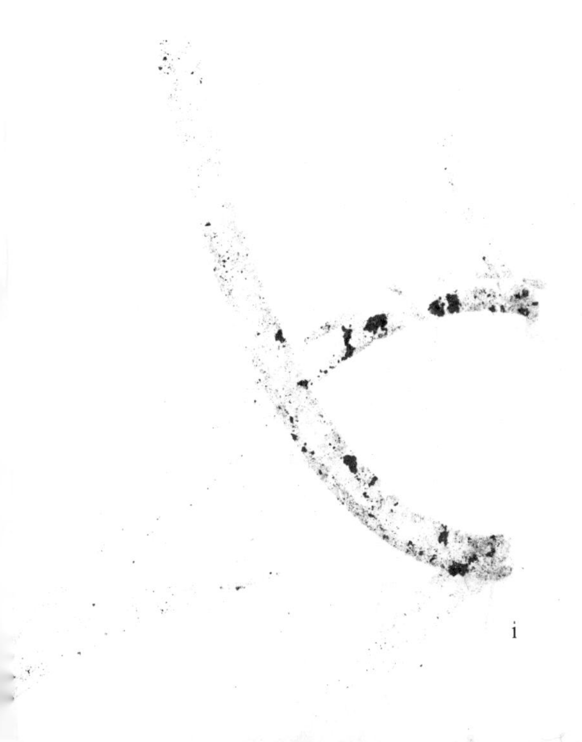

ISBN:
ISBN-13:

LEGAL DISCLAIMER: Jack Rosenthal does not guarantee the success of any of the ideas or suggestions in this book. Further, no representations are made as to the accuracy of any information contained herein, including without limitation dollar amounts, percentages, profit estimates, sales estimates and the like. In addition, the extent permitted by law, Jack Rosenthal shall not be responsible for any losses and/or damages due to the use of the information or suggestions in this book, ebook, or any reproduction in any form. Names of the companies or people mentioned herein do not necessarily reflect actual names or titles. By reading beyond this point you hereby consent to this disclaimer and agree to its terms.

Table of Contents

CHAPTER ONE

THE ULTIMATE GUIDE TO TEEN INVESTING

As a teenager, I've now been investing for almost 10 years in the equity and debt markets. I'm the Founder and President of the Young Investors Club, LLC, one of the largest teen-run investment groups in the country with nearly 100 members and over $117,000 in assets under management. Over the past 10 years I've made and witnessed hundreds of trades in both my own and the group's portfolio. I've seen firsthand what it takes to be a good investor, a combination of luck and skill, and have generated $20,000+ in gains. All throughout I've maintained a few key principles which I've used to generate wealth for myself and the hundreds of other teenagers and young investors I teach. Throughout this book I will share those principles as well as general rules and guidelines any teen or adult should refer to when investing.

Investopedia defines investing as "The act of allocating funds to an asset or committing capital to an endeavor (a business, project, fund, etc.), with the expectation of generating an income or profit."

The keyword in this definition is "expectation." Investing is not a guaranteed bet; like any bet there is the chance you will lose some or all of your investment. The risk of an investment generally determines the return, hence you may have heard the phrase "the higher the risk the higher the reward." If you keep your money in the bank you are virtually taking no risk and as long your accounts remains under $250k it is insured by the U.S. Federal Government. Because of the extremely low risk you're taking, you're getting a very small reward of about 1% based on current interest rates.

Now on the opposite extreme, if you were to provide seed capital to an early venture with a high risk of failure, like investing in Amazon.com while Jeff Bezos was running it out of his garage, you could earn a return of over 5000% on your money. In fact, had you invested $1000 in Amazon on its IPO date it would be worth $1,340,000 today. What an amazing bet that would have been, but of course that doesn't account for the 999,999 other investors who invested in similar ventures which ended up failing causing them to lose their entire investment. Dating back to the Dutch East India Company (the first publicly traded stock), which financed merchant ships on trade voyages, investing has always been about the risk you're taking in exchange for the potential reward you're getting.

Not investing is itself a risk. Due to inflation (a general increase in prices over time), $1 today is worth more than $1 tomorrow. This is an extreme example but it's meant to illustrate the point that your money loses value over time. The $100 you keep in your drawer won't have the same purchasing power of $100 today in 10 years; in fact at current inflation rates, $100 will only be worth the equivalent to $79.37 10 years from now. You'll still have that $100 bill in 10 years but it will only be able to buy $79.37 worth of items. So by not investing your money, you're essentially losing money every year.

How much money do you need to start investing? This is a question I get all the time from my friends and peers. Now keep in mind that the answer to this question is a very arbitrary number and there are a lot of factors involved including your age, what part of the world you live in and what your income goals are etc. Also, a 100% logical investment advisor would tell you to begin investing with any amount, however ultimately I think we can agree that earning $0.40/year on a $10 investment is simply not worth the effort.

For teenagers aged 13-18 I would generally advise you start investing with no less than $1000. Even though the initial return on your investment may be small (you can expect between $50 and $100 per year) it's still a great way to start learning about investing, and there's no better way to learn about investing then actually practicing it. However, if your goal in investing is to use the profits to pay for part of your livelihood, I would recommend starting your investment portfolio with no less than a $5000 initial investment; that way the profits from your investments (expect $250-$500/year) are significant enough to pay for some expenses.

Before I forget to mention it, checkout this link to get signed up for my Teen Investing Newsletter > https://bit.ly/TeenInvestingNewsletter.

CHAPTER TWO

HOW TO EARN MONEY TO INVEST?

I know this is an investing book, but you simply can't invest unless you have the funds to invest in the first place, there's no way around it. You can try out one of the mock portfolios - one of the best ones I've used is Market Watch (https://www.marketwatch.com/game);

However, it doesn't simulate the feelings and emotions involved in actual investing, not to mention the real-life profits gained. Say your goal was to start with an investment portfolio worth $5000. Now I know that's no small amount of money, that's probably more than your Xbox, phone, computer, and spare spending cash all combined. However, it is by no means unattainable. I'm not saying there won't be hard work involved but if you're really committed to start building wealth at an early age, you can make it happen. And remember, as a teenager, now is the best time to start earning money because you have virtually no expenses - which means all the money you earn can go directly into savings.

How to earn more money?

Here is a list of 15 jobs/businesses you can start today!

1) **Babysitting** - probably the most iconic teenage job. Though I've never babysat before, I've heard from my friends who do, that it's not too hard a gig. You'll earn $10-$20/hour to hang out with a kid for a few hours and then watch TV for a few more hours after he or she goes to sleep — not a bad way to earn money.

2) **Local Town Job** - Of the 10-30 businesses in your town right now, I'm sure one of them is looking for a teen employee. Try asking your local sushi restaurant, Italian restaurant, supermarket, ice cream shop, barbershop/nail salon, toy store, pizza place, or gym; I bet one of them has a job waiting for you!

3) **Tech Repair and Set-Up**- If you have a knack for computers or coding, starting your own computer repair business could be a great idea. Tons of adults and elders have the money to buy the latest technology, computers, TV's, Speakers, etc. but have no clue what to do when it comes to the setup process or what to do if their technology stops working. As a teenager, you could charge up to $50-$75/hour for house calls. If you're looking to get into the business, I would recommend putting out flyers around your town as well as telling your family and friends to patronize your business as its first few clients to get the business off the ground.

4) **Lawn Mowing / Snow Blowing**- The tried and true lawn mowing business has been written about for years; however there still remains a heavy

demand for it. You can make some extra cash this summer by simply knocking on all your nearby neighbors' doors and offering to cut their grass. This business does require an initial investment of buying a lawnmower; however I believe you can get a used one for a small $300-$400 investment. You can apply the same strategy and provide snow blowing / snow shoveling services for nearby neighbors on snow days as well.

5) **Vending Machine** - I do have some personal experience in this business. When I was 13-years old I bought my first Vending Machine. A used vending machine typically costs anywhere from $800-$3000 so it does require a large upfront investment; however, if you find the right location, they can be quite profitable for a minimal amount of effort required. Think about it, a vending machine is the perfect business, it's like running your own mini store with no employee or rent costs. A vending machine in a solid location can earn $50-$100 per week. Some of the locations you might want to first approach are factories/warehouses, hotels/inns, auto body shops, office buildings, and any other high traffic locations. You also don't necessarily need to buy the standard snack vending machine to get started. You can start off small by buying a gumball machine for $200-$300 or simply by buying an honor box for $30-$70. An honor box is essentially a snack box where you leave snacks in a box and trust people to leave money in the slip of the box. You might want to place one of these in an area where people often wait, like a nail salon or a barbershop. Based on my assumptions, you can probably make

$10 a week running one of these. Vending machines overall are great businesses for young adults and teens to operate, you just need to make sure you find a good location before buying one!

6) **E-commerce** - Opening an online store to sell products is easier than ever nowadays. If you have a product to sell, which can be anything from handmade soap to electronics you buy in bulk and then resell individually you can set up an online shop relatively quickly. If you're looking to sell your products on your own site, I would recommend Shopify.com, however if you're looking to sell your products on platforms which already have large user bases, I would recommend Amazon, eBay and Etsy. In my freshmen year I caught on to the fidget spinner trend early and sold fidget spinners on Ebay.com. I sold over $1000 worth of fidget spinners in that year alone. Lesson - catch on to trends early and monetize them.

7) **Tutoring** - If you're a good student, I strongly recommend tutoring. Often you can undercut traditional tutoring services by at least 50%, and as a student yourself you probably know the material even better than the conventional tutors.

8) **House Cleaning** - Cleaning other people's houses is a great way to earn some additional income. If you're able to get your customers to sign up for monthly cleaning, you can build a real business with consistent recurring monthly revenue.

9) **Influencer** - Being a Youtuber, Blogger, or Instagrammer (not sure if that's a word) I would all put under the general category of being an

influencer. If you're able to build a sizeable audience on any of these platforms you can start to monetize your pages, whether that be through putting ads on your YouTube channel or blog or through getting paid by brands to promote products on your Instagram feed. Being an influencer is also a great way to get tons of free stuff in exchange for promoting products/services to your audience.

10) **Photography** - If you're good with a camera and own one, you can start your own photography business. Some good niches to get into are wedding photography, event photography, portrait photographer and my personal favorite real estate photography for local realtors in your area.

11) **Baking Business**- If you have a knack for baking, you can offer to sell your pastries to other bakeshops, friends, and family members for special events, or at local town fairs and flea markets where people can pay for bite-size portions of baked goods.

12) **Jewelry** - Making your own custom jewelry that can be sold in jewelry stores and online is a great way to combine business with something you're passionate about. You can also sell jewelry on platforms like Etsy (an online website made just for handmade goods) as well as promote your product line on Instagram.

13) **Sell Products for Others** - A lot of people have old technology and items sitting around their house they don't use or don't need. However, the process of listing a product on a site like eBay and waiting around for offers can sometimes be too much of a

hassle for busy adults. That's why you can offer to sell people's own products for them on eBay and charge them anywhere from 20%-50% of the selling price if the item sells.

14) **Flipping** - One of my favorite online entrepreneurs Gary Vee talks about the garage sale hustle where he drives out to garage sales, buys products for extremely undervalued prices, and sells them for their true values on eBay. This may seem too good to be true; however if you know how to negotiate and research on eBay for the true values of items, it's not that hard to earn $75-$100 per weekend garage sale flipping. It is not just products you find at garage sales that can be flipped, you can also flip rare or novelty items you know a lot about, whether they are limited edition shoes, trading cards, or rare coins.

15) **Dog Walking** - Adults make entire careers out of dog walking. Some professional dog walkers make between $30,000 to $80,000/year. Of the people you know, how many of them have dogs? It's not that hard a market to tap into… The average dog walker charges around $20 a walk, so if you can convince 5 dog owners to let you walk their dogs every week, you can make an extra $100 a week for a little over an hour's worth of work.

Bonus - Web Design - Being a web designer doesn't even require advanced coding knowledge nowadays. Typically, web hosting services like WIX and GoDaddy have pre-laid out templates you can just drag and drop photos and text into. Web development is a great way to earn an income without having to leave your house. You can list your services for sale on sites like Fiverr.com and Upwork as well as many other freelance sites and offer fixed rates to create fully custom websites for people and businesses. Teenage web designers can typically charge anywhere from $250-$1000 per website.

If anyone of these paid $15 an hour (the minimum wage in my home state of New York) and you worked 10 hours a week (5 during the week and 5 on weekends) you could save over $5000 in less than a year!

CHAPTER THREE

WHAT ARE STOCKS AND BONDS?

Stocks The very first stock ever created was the Dutch East India Company which issued its first share of stock in 1602. The Dutch didn't know it then but they were making the first steps in creating a multi-trillion-dollar financial market that touches each and every one of us whether we know it or not. Some of the most popular consumer products you buy and consume on an everyday basis from Starbucks coffee (SBUX) to Ketchup (HEINZ) to Facebook (FB) are all publicly traded stocks. Stocks are "an equity investment that represents part ownership in a corporation and entitles you to part of that corporation's earnings and assets." However, simply speaking, a share of stock is a piece of a company. The potential reward in buying stocks is immense because if you own stock in a company and that company increases in value you are a direct recipient of that increase in value. The risk you're taking in buying stock is, unlike bonds, when you buy a share of stock, the company is not obligated to pay you back any or part of your investment.

Bonds, on the other hand, are required to pay you back your full investment plus interest. A bond is essentially a loan with a preset annual interest payment. The value of bonds increase and decrease on a day to day basis however, not nearly by the same significant percentages that stocks do. Safer, larger companies such as Apple typically pay around 3-4% annually on their bonds, whereas smaller riskier bonds (often referred to as junk bonds) can pay up to 7% to 8% on their bonds.

Because of the higher risk involved in owning a piece of a company (remember what I said in the beginning about risk vs. reward) as opposed to debt against it, stocks generally pay a higher return over long periods of time. Although the S&P 500 (a collection of the 500 largest U.S. stocks) is volatile - some years it could be up 20%, while other years it could be down 20%, over time the S&P 500 has generally produced between an 8-10% return annualized, significantly greater than the majority of bonds investors can ever expect to earn. Conclusion? In the long run, Stocks are generally far better investments for teenagers because your investment portfolio lifespan is significantly longer. Teens can afford to wait out the highs and lows and let their portfolios steadily grow over time without the immediate need to withdraw funds.

Preferred Stock

Preferred stock is a more "senior" ownership of the company compared to common stock. That simply means that these shares get paid first. Owners of preferred stock have a higher claim to dividends than common stock which is what most people refer to when referencing stocks. Typically, preferred stock pays a fixed dividend on a monthly or quarterly basis. Because preferred stock owners assume less risk (they are higher on the capital structure if the company were to go bankrupt and would be paid back their investment first before common stockholders) they also can expect a lower return.

You can generally make a return of between 4-6% investing in preferred stocks. They are normally issued by banks, utility companies and real estate investment trusts (REITS) which receive cashflow on a consistent monthly or quarterly basis.

Options

Options are a financial derivative. An option gives the buyer or seller of the option the right to buy or sell an asset by a certain time and price in the future.

Call options – these options allow the holder to buy an asset a specific price (called the strike price) within a specific time period.

Put options – these options allow the holder to sell an asset at a specific price within a specific time period.

All options eventually expire if they are not used within a specific time frame.

The key thing to remember about options is they give the owners the right, but not the obligation, to sell or buy the stock at the agreed upon strike price.

How do they work?

Each buyer of an option pays the seller something called a "premium" for the right to buy or sell their stock at an agreed upon price before an agreed upon time.

Option contracts are usually traded in 100 share increments. For example, to buy call options on the S&P 500 (ticker: IVV) which is currently trading at $320 you would need to pay approximately 0.80% of that amount for the right to hold an option for a one-month period. However, since the contracts are for 100 shares each, you need to buy 100x at a time so that would be a total of $256 ($320*.008*100). So, if you bought one option contract for $256 and the IVV went up 1.25% that month you would double your money. The reason why you can generate such a high return is because of leverage. That 1.25% is compounded by 100x because your option contract gives you the right to the gains on 100 shares So, for 100 shares at $256 which is a total position of $32,000 (of buying power) a 1.25% increase in share price that month would turn your $256 into approximately $512.

In order to be a covered call option seller, you would need to hold at least 100 shares of one stock. To use the IVV as an example again, your total position would need to be $32,000 (100 shares x $320 per share). By selling the same options contracts I detailed for 0.8% of the total share value in premiums you would be giving up any rights to any increase in value for that month. However, you would be gaining a .8% return on your investment that month. If you did this every month of the year you would earn a 9.6% return, even if the stock market remained flat for the whole year.

*All numbers are approximately correct.

Index Funds

In a relatively short time, index funds have become the #1 investment vehicle for passive investors. Index funds are great ways to invest in the stock market without being forced to put in a lot of time and effort into picking the right stocks or having to pay heavy fees like traditional funds would charge. As noted earlier, the S&P 500 is an Index fund which has had an average annual return of 9.8%, so by investing in the S&P 500 index fund; you are capturing that same return without being forced to put any effort or time into choosing individual stocks. It's also a much safer way to invest in the stock market due to the diversification it offers.

Diversification is a common strategy investors use to minimize risk by making smaller investments in many different investments as opposed to a single large investment in one company. Unlike investing in just a few stocks, investing in the S&P 500 allows you to spread out your risk across many companies throughout many different industries. Lastly, there is a huge fee advantage to investing in Vanguard index funds. Unlike a traditional fund that could charge as high as 2% of your total investment as well as 20%

of the profits they produce, index funds typically charge a flat fee of just 0.20% of your assets. Lower fees mean more leftover profits for the investor (you). Overall I believe investing in indexes is the #1 way a passive investor can generate a strong return with little to no effort required.

What I look for in Stock Investments?

How do you decide which stocks to invest in? Over the years I've heard dozens of different strategies and theories on how to choose stocks but there are no "known" strategies that consistently perform above the market return (the S&P 500 return of 9.8%). There are many different metrics investors use such as P/E ratios, PEG ratios, dividends, market caps, insider holdings and many more and I will discuss in detail what all of them mean. However, there is no single best strategy one can use to guarantee to make money in the stock market. That being said there are two fundamental strategies that have worked for my investors and me over the years.

1) Do you believe in the company and its longevity? When looking at a stock, you are really looking at the company, and often you are a direct or indirect consumer of that company's goods and services. When I invest in stocks I first want to make sure I believe in the product, the company is simple to understand, and I genuinely think the company will exist over the next 20 years. I like to look for boring, predictable and most importantly safe companies.

An example of one of these companies is Con Ed, a utility that provides power to the New York area. For the most part it has a monopoly on the electrical power grid and electricity is a resource that is a need for virtually every single household in the New York metropolitan area. This meets all three checks. One it's simple to understand; they produce and transport power to households and businesses in New York. Two, it's boring, electricity production isn't a very exciting business and it is unlikely there will be any major breakthroughs that will allow me to make 10x my money in the next few years; however, electricity isn't going anywhere anytime soon either. Electricity usage still continues to rise at a steady rate every year due to the increased reliance on technology in almost all facets of life. Lastly, I do believe Con Ed will be around for at least the next 20 years if not more due to their essential monopoly over all the power lines that feed into the homes and businesses of millions of people.

2) Is it the right time? Timing is everything. Con Ed, for example, I believe is an amazing company; however, if I don't purchase the company at the right time and buy the stock at the right price I could easily overpay for it and lose part of my investment. Timing in the stock market is possibly more important than the company itself.

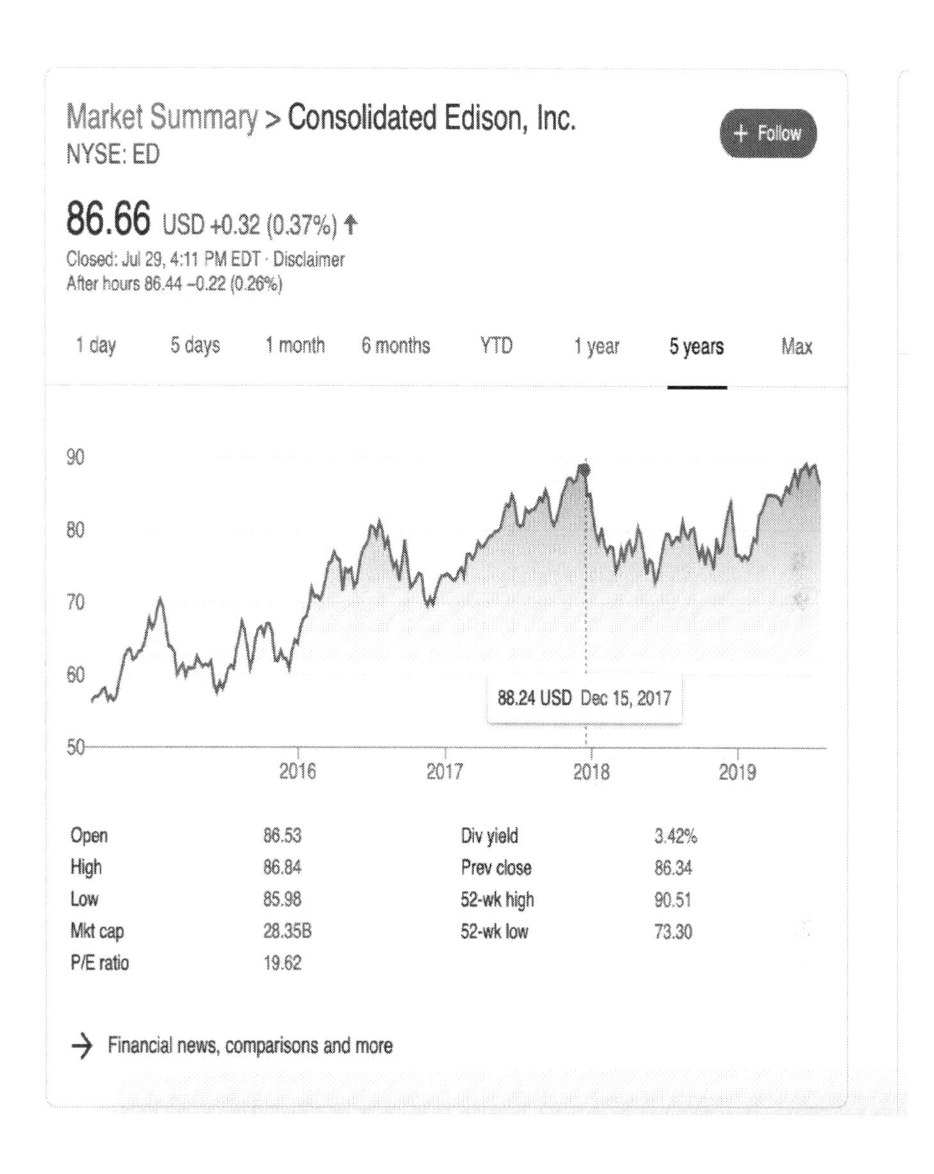

For this particular stock, I might wait to invest until there is a dip in the share price again, especially if that dip is caused by an event that I don't think will affect the company's long term profits (like a power outage). Not to mention, the company pays a solid dividend of 3.42% per year. I will explain what dividends are later but they are essentially an annual interest rate the company pays you to hold the stock.

How I find companies

One of the best ways I choose the stocks in my own portfolio is by first looking for companies I believe in and I think are here to stay. After I've compiled a list of 20 or so of these companies, I'll look at the current 1-year and 5-year chart of each stock. The first thing I avoid is 5 years of negative growth such as Deutsche Bank stock. The company's consistent 5 years of market value loss is simply too great a risk to take on when considering purchasing the stock. Take a look at the chart below.

However, 5+ years of positive growth such as another one of my favorites (WM) is a very positive sign of long term performance.

Amazon.com, Inc Yahoo Finance

CHAPTER FOUR

THE METRICS

There are literally thousands of different metrics investors use to measure the performance of a company; however I will highlight only the two dozen or so I believe to be the most important and will help you analyze any stocks you may be considering. The best way to do this is with a case study for a single stock using the Yahoo finance portal (https://finance.yahoo.com).

Let's use Amazon as an example. As I'm sure you know, Amazon is the #1 e-commerce company in the world and also owns numerous other businesses such as AWS Amazon Web Services, and numerous physical product lines such as Amazon basic and Ring. In this chapter, I will show and explain to you what all the various metrics on Yahoo finance mean and how to interpret each of them.

The first page that will come when you type in any stock's name into the search bar is the summary page.

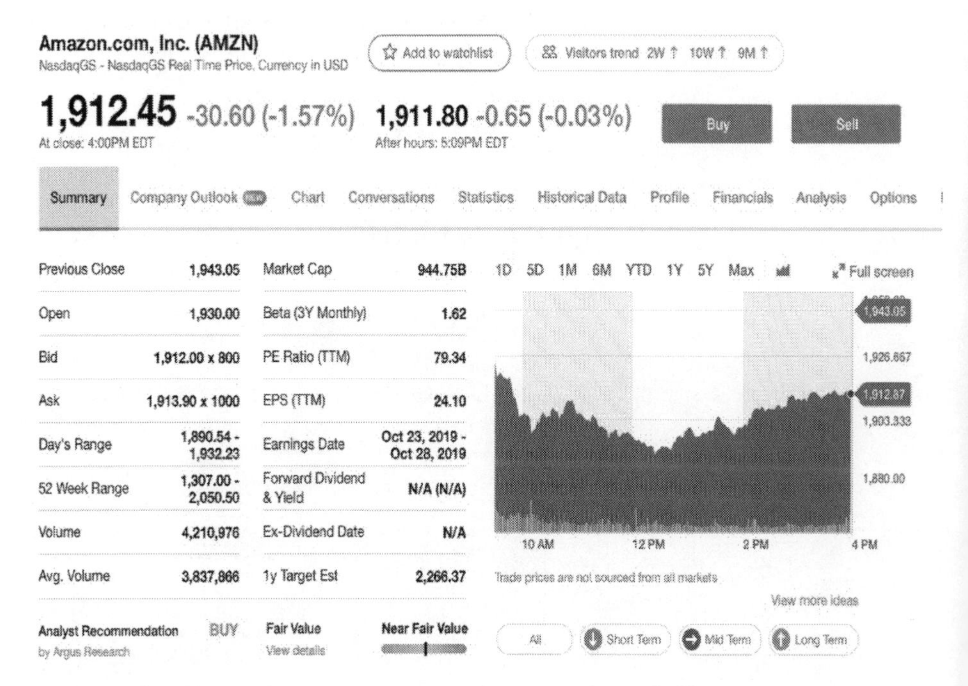

We'll make our way down the different terms vertically

1) The $1912.45 is the price or current value of each share. The -1.57% represents how much the stock decreased or increased since the last previous closing price of the stock.

2) Previous close price of $1943.05 is the last price of the share at the close of the stock market from the previous business day. The stock market is open from 9:30am to 4:00pm.

3) The "Open" is the first price the stock traded at the beginning of trading during the current day (9:30am).

4) The Bid and the Ask are what make up the price

of the stock. The bid is the highest price a buyer is willing to pay per share at that exact moment and the ask is the lowest price a seller is willing to sell their shares at that exact moment. Usually, there is a very small difference between the two (known as the "spread"); the last buyers and sellers last agreed to make a trade that determines the stock's current price.

5) Day's Range is the highest and lowest price the stock traded at during the day.

6) 52 Week Range is the highest and lowest price the stock traded at during the last year (52 weeks)

7) Volume is the number of total shares that exchanged hands at the most recent trading day.

8) Average Volume is the average number of shares traded on a typical day. So if there was a large spike above the average on a certain day, there was likely a large news event that caused the increase in trading (Either positive or negative news can both affect this metric)

9) Market cap is the total equity value of the company. Another way to calculate that is by multiplying the total number of shares outstanding, which for Amazon is (492,332,000) by the price per share $1912.45 and you'll get $941.5 billion.

10) Beta is the stock's overall volatility as compared to the market as a whole.

11) P/E Ratio is one of the most important metrics to look at when evaluating a stock. It gives you a ratio of the price (or market cap) of the company relative to the earnings of the company. For example, if you ran a company and it produced $100 profit and an Investor was willing to pay and 8 P/E ratio for your company, it would then be worth $800. Based on Amazon's P/E ratio of 80, investors are willing to pay 80 times the current annual earnings of Amazon. Why do stocks go for ridiculous high values such as these? It's because investors believe companies like Amazon and others will have such high earnings in the future and because of that their investment will really have a more reasonable 10 to 15 price to earnings ratio in the future. The average P/E ratio of the SPY 500 over the last 100+ years has been 15.77

12) EPS or earnings per share is the total amount of earnings divided by all the shares of the company. So by Amazon's current P/E ratio of 80x the earnings per share is $24.10 and you're paying over 80x that to purchase one share.

13) Earnings date is the last date the earnings of the company were reported.

14) Forward Dividend yield is the current dividend divided by the stock price. A dividend is the earnings paid out to shareholders on a quarterly, monthly or annual basis (typically quarterly). Think of it as the cash flow from a business. If you paid $100 for a stock and it pays all its

investors a $5 dividend per year, you are earning a dividend yield of 5%. This category is blank for Amazon because Amazon doesn't pay a dividend. It takes that $24 in earnings it would otherwise pay its investors for owning its stock and reinvests it back into the business to hopefully grow the company even larger.

15) Ex-dividend date is the first date that the stock trades without the dividend. In other words, if you buy the shares on the ex-dividend date, you will not receive the dividend; if you buy the shares the day before the ex-dividend date, you will receive the dividend.

16) 1-year target est is the price per share that some analysts think the company will be worth in one year

The "Chart" Tab allows you to see a list of all the prices of the stock traded at over different lengths of time. I have selected the "1 Year Price Chart" which shows all the prices Amazon traded at going back 1 year from the day the chart was captured.

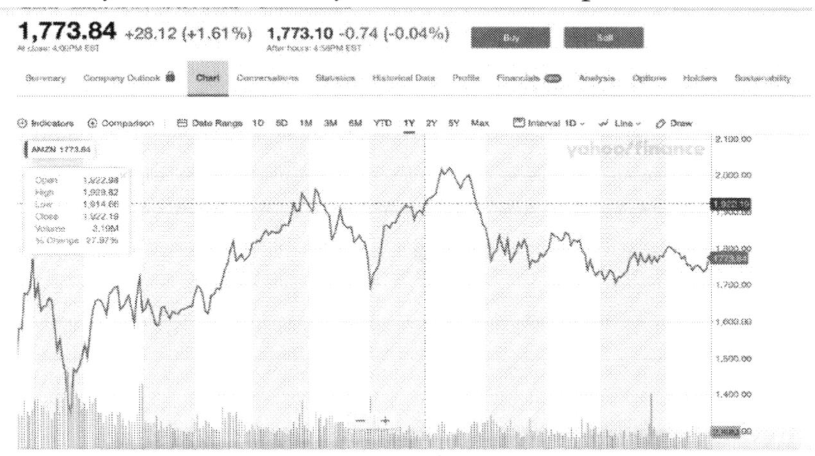

Amazon.com, Inc Yahoo Finance

It also allows you to compare one stock to another by clicking "comparison."

Here I compared Amazon to Google over the last year. The compassion feature is a good tool to use if you're measuring the performance of two companies in a similar industry.

The "Conversations" tab is a cool way to see what other investors are saying about the stock in real-time.

The "Statistics" Tab explains:

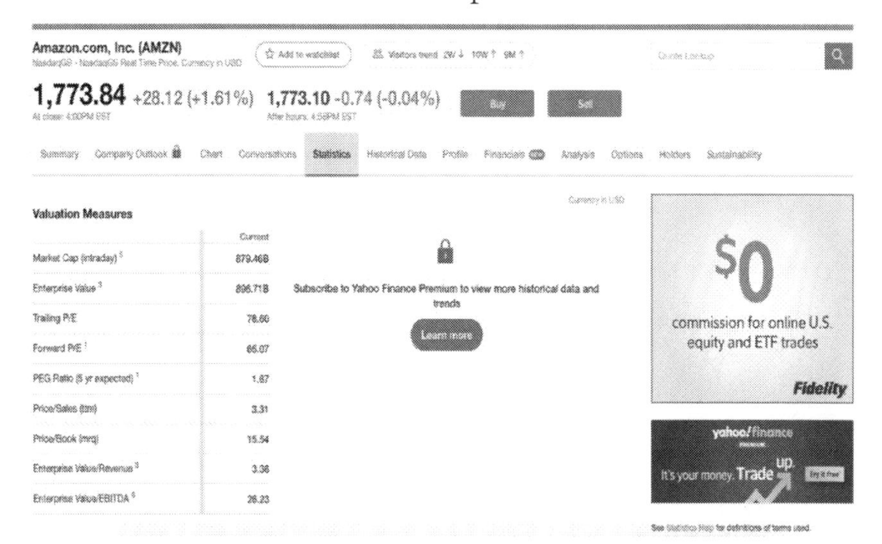

Amazon.com, Inc Yahoo Finance

1. **Market Cap** - (previously covered)

2. **Enterprise Value** is an alternative to using the market cap to value a company. It includes the market cap but also includes the debt the company has as well as the cash the company has.

3. **Trailing P/E** - (previously covered).

4. **Forward P/E** - this is the price (or total market cap of the company) divided by the predicted earnings over the next 12 months.

5. **PEG (5 years)** - is the company's P/E ratio divided by its growth rate over the last 5 years. This metric is more important than the P/E ratio for high growth

companies like Amazon because it factors in growth as well.

6. **Price/Sales ttm** - is the market cap of the company divided by the sales or revenue of the company in the last 12 months.

7. **Price/Book mrq** is the market cap divided by the book value. The book value is the net asset value of the company which is total tangible assets subtracted by total liabilities.

8. **Enterprise Value/Revenue** is pretty self-explanatory, it is the enterprise value divided by the total revenue of the company.

9. **Enterprise Value/EBITDA** - This is the Enterprise Value divided by EBITDA

10. **EBITDA** - EBITDA could be one of the most quoted and single most important numbers in modern finance. It's a simple equation:

    Earnings Before Interest, Tax, Depreciation and Amortization.

    Earnings - the net profits of the company

    Interest - The interest the company is paying on its outstanding debt

    Tax - Taxes the company owes

    Depreciation - The amount of an asset value that the company has already used. For example, if I bought a truck for $10,000 and I knew I could get 100,000 miles out of the truck before it broke down and I could no longer use it, I would subtract the proportionate amount of miles I already used from the value of the car to determine the true value of the car. If I ran a supply route and I used my truck to drive 30,000 miles that year I would subtract $3,000 (as depreciation) from my earnings that year while I was operating the company because although I did not spend $3,000 I might as well have through the used up mileage in the car.

Amortization - Amortization is debt repayments on the principle of debt a company holds. For example, if a company borrowed $1000 and their debt holder requested they pay $200 of the principal (the $1000) back each year plus interest, the $200 would represent the Amortization.

EBITDA is often used by investors to paint a very good picture of how much operating income a company produces and thus is a key metric used in determining the value of public and private companies.

Quick Definitions

Public Company - A public company is a company traded on the stock exchange that is open to the "public" for anyone to buy.

Private Company – A private company is a company that is held under "private" ownership.

The "Profile" section shows a list of the company's key executives as well as provides an in-depth description of what the company does.

Amazon.com, Inc Yahoo Finance

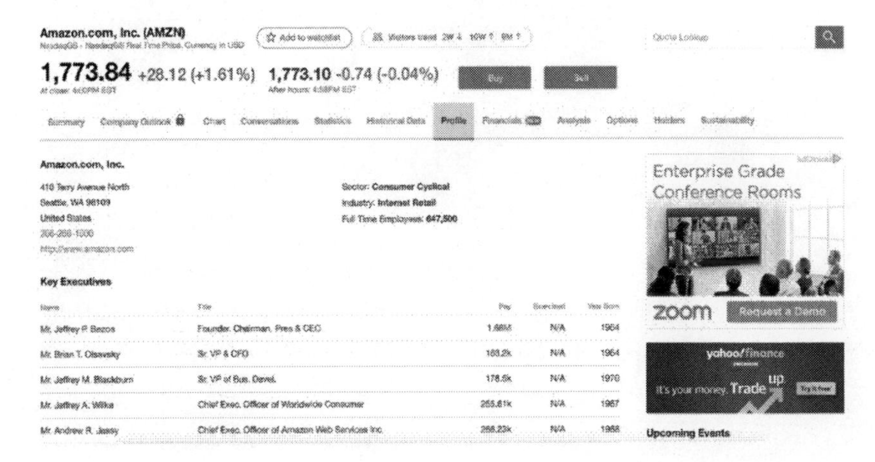

Description

Amazon.com, Inc. engages in the retail sale of consumer products and subscriptions in North America and internationally. The company operates through three segments: North America, International, and Amazon Web Services (AWS) segments. It sells merchandise and content purchased for resale from third-party sellers through physical stores and online stores. The company also manufactures and sells electronic devices, including Kindle e-readers, Fire tablets, Fire TVs, and Echo devices; provides Kindle Direct Publishing, an online service that allows independent authors and publishers to make their books available in the Kindle Store; and develops and produces media content, as well as offers Echo Flex, a plug-in smart speaker. In addition, it offers programs that enable sellers to sell their products on its Websites, as well as their own branded Websites; and programs that allow authors, musicians, filmmakers, skill and app developers, and others to publish and sell content. Further, the company provides compute, storage, database, and other AWS services, as well as compute, storage, database offerings, fulfillment, publishing, digital content subscriptions, advertising, and co-branded credit card agreement services. Additionally, it offers Amazon Prime, a membership program, which provides free shipping of various items; access to streaming of movies and TV episodes; and other services. It serves consumers, sellers, developers, enterprises, and content creators. Amazon.com, Inc. has a strategic partnership with Volkswagen AG. The company was founded in 1994 and is headquartered in Seattle, Washington.

Of all these metric here are the top 3 my grandfather and I use to analyze stocks

1. P/E Ratio

The P/E ratio is the first metric we look at. Typically P/E ratios of large companies that make up the U.S. Stock Market are anywhere from 12-50. However, Amazon's is currently over 76. Why? Because Investors predict that Amazon's future earnings will be even greater than its past earnings. They are effectively willing to pay more for the company because they believe it will make more and therefore be worth more in the future. We generally like to invest in companies whose future P/E ratios, based on how much we think the company will earn, will be between 10-15.

2. PEG Ratio The PEG Ratio is often used as a counter to the P/E Ratio. The Price to Earnings Growth Ratio is used to take projected growth into account (just like the Amazon example I previously discussed). You calculate it by dividing the P/E ratio by the company's expected growth rate. For example a company with a 20 P/E ratio and a 10% growth rate would have a PEG ratio of 2.0. In general companies with PEG ratios below 1 are considered to be undervalued while companies with PEG ratios above 1 are considered to be overvalued. However, for very high growth companies at the forefront of their industries, like Amazon, its reasonable to expect a PEG ratio greater than 1. Amazon currently has a PEG ratio of 2.91 significantly higher than the E-commerce industry's average of 1.30.

3. Debt to Equity

The D/E ratio is the ratio of the company's debt (borrowed assets) to its equity (assets). A Lower Debt to Equity ratio means the company needs a lower amount of debt to finance its investments. Toys R Us is a prime example of a company that recently went out of business largely because of a high Debt to Equity ratio. Toys R Us towards the end of its existence had a D/E ratio of 78% Debt to 22% Equity. Nearly 3x more debt than equity. We generally like to steer clear of companies with huge amounts of debt relative to their equity.

CHAPTER FIVE

SAVINGS

As a teenager or young adult, I would recommend contributing 60-70% of your income (after tax) to your investment portfolio. Your income as a teenager is essentially all pure profit, as you have no expenses! Rent, food, insurance, clothing are all FREE. Besides perhaps gas money and a few other minor expenses all the other places you spend your money are essentially luxuries you don't need. Save as much money early on as you can because it won't be as easy to do when you're older.

CHAPTER SIX

WHY BEING YOUNG IS THE BEST TIME TO BE AN INVESTOR?

Being a teenager is among one of the best times to get started in investing because as a teenager, you possess certain luxuries that you just don't have as an adult.

1) **You have virtually no expenses.** Expenses quite literally disintegrate investment portfolios. Rent/housing, food, clothing, insurance, car payments, home renovations/maintenance, electricity, and the list goes on, are all FREE. As a teenager you have the unique ability to create an investment portfolio and build wealth entirely uninterrupted by the bills and expenses of everyday life.

2) **You have time on your side**. Time is one of the best fuels to grow an investment portfolio because of a force called compound interest. Albert Einstein once said "Compound interest is the 8th wonder of the world. He who understands it earns it; he who doesn't, pays it." Compound interest is the interest you earn on the interest + principal of your deposit or in other words interest on top of interest. It might

not sound like there's a huge difference between earning 8% compounded on your money for 10 years vs 20 years but there is. Investing $100,000 over 10 years will earn you $215,892.50 vs 20 years will earn you $466,095.71. Time is one of the largest factors in growing investment portfolios. The longer you have to invest the more time it gives your money to grow and compound.

CHAPTER SEVEN

BOND METRICS

I've mostly discussed stocks; however, it's important to address bonds and how to analyze them. Here are a few key terms any bond investor should know.

Bond Terms

i. **Face value** - is the amount that the bond will be worth upon the final date on which the loan is due.

ii. **Coupon rate** - is the interest rate that the bond issuer will pay the lenders

iii. **Maturity date** - is the final date upon which the bond is due.

iv. **Issue pric**e - is the current price of the bond. Prices move according to the certainty the market has that the bond issuer will be able to repay the bond.

CHAPTER EIGHT

YAHOO FINANCE: DEEP DIVE

How to View the Financial Statement of a Company

1) Go to https://finance.yahoo.com

2) Enter your stock into the search bar

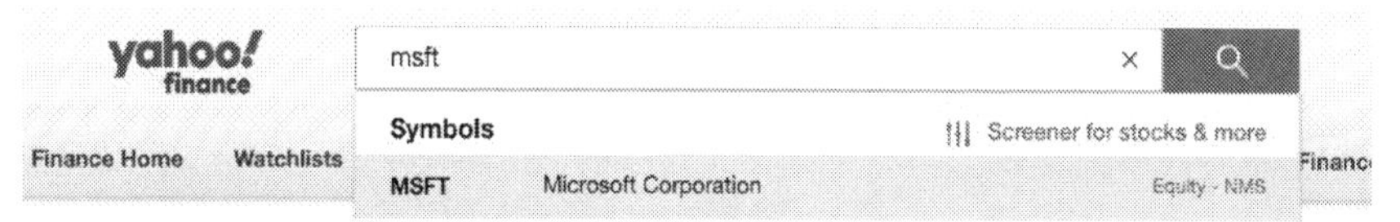

3) Click "Financials"

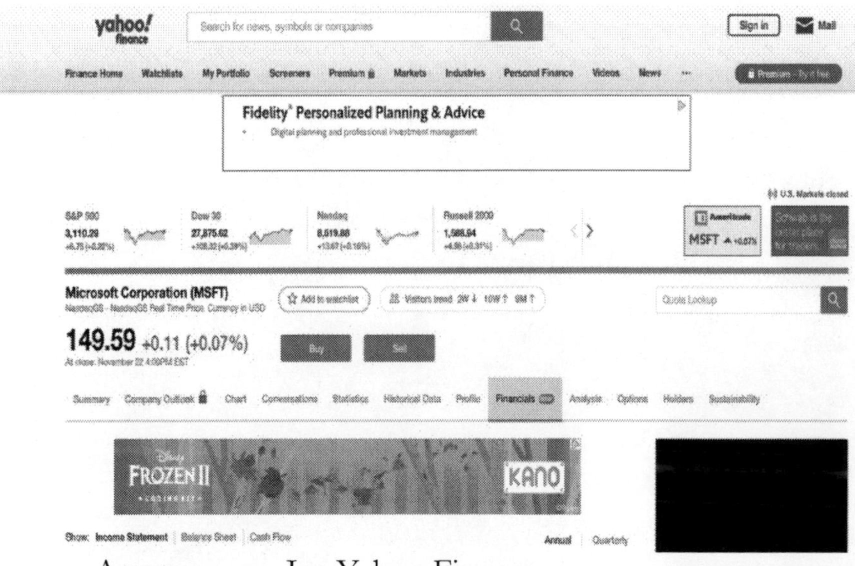

Amazon.com, Inc Yahoo Finance

4) View Summary:

We'll start at the top then make our way down

Breakdown	TTM	9/29/2019	9/29/2018	9/29/2017	9/29/2016
Total Revenue	259,034,000	260,174,000	265,595,000	229,234,000	215,639,000
Cost of Revenue	160,871,000	161,782,000	163,756,000	141,048,000	131,376,000
Gross Profit	98,163,000	98,392,000	101,839,000	88,186,000	84,263,000
v Operating Expenses					
Research Development	15,857,000	16,217,000	14,236,000	11,581,000	10,045,000
Selling General and Administrative	17,883,000	18,245,000	16,705,000	15,261,000	14,194,000
Total Operating Expenses	33,740,000	34,462,000	30,941,000	26,842,000	24,239,000
Operating Income or Loss	64,423,000	63,930,000	70,898,000	61,344,000	60,024,000
Interest Expense	3,634,000	-	3,240,000	2,323,000	1,456,000
Total Other Income/Expenses Net	76,000	1,807,000	2,005,000	2,745,000	1,348,000
Income Before Tax	66,031,000	65,737,000	72,903,000	64,089,000	61,372,000
Income Tax Expense	10,336,000	10,481,000	13,372,000	15,738,000	15,685,000
Income from Continuing Operations	55,695,000	55,256,000	59,531,000	48,351,000	45,687,000
Net Income	55,695,000	55,256,000	59,531,000	48,351,000	45,687,000
Net Income available to common s...	55,695,000	55,256,000	59,531,000	48,351,000	45,687,000
v Reported EPS					
Basic	-	-	12.01	9.27	8.35
Diluted	-	-	11.91	9.21	8.31
v Weighted average shares outst...					
Basic	-	-	4,955,377	5,217,242	5,470,820
Diluted	-	-	5,000,109	5,251,692	5,500,281
EBITDA	-	76,477,000	81,801,000	71,501,000	70,529,000

TTM - Trailing 12 months (in other words 12 months back starting from the current month)

Total Revenue - The amount of money the company takes in total from selling its good and/or services

Cost of Revenue - Many times referred to as the

cost of goods. In other words, if I had a widget and it cost me $2 for the raw materials of that widget, that $2 would be my cost of revenue.

Gross Profit - The amount of money the company earns after the cost of its product. For example, if you ran a company which sold widgets and you sold them for $10 while it costs you $2 for the raw materials your gross profit would be $8, however, this does not take into account other costs such as labor, rent for your factory, and many other auxiliary expenses.

Research and Development - The amount of money a company spends on developing new products and perfecting its existing product.

Selling General and Administrative Services - This is the company's labor costs for everyone involved in running the company

Operating Income or Loss - This is the company's final "operating" income after you take into account the cost of revenue, research and development, and selling.

Selling General and Administrative Services - This is the **Most** Important line I look at when evaluating a company's financial statement because it gives you a very good idea of how much profit the company is generating.

The rest of the expenses are somewhat tax-related and not as important to the health of the company (unless they have a lot of debt on their balance sheet).

CHAPTER NINE

HOW I FOUNDED THE WORLD'S LARGEST TEEN INVESTMENT ORGANIZATION.

By September of my freshman year, I'd been investing in the stock market alongside my grandfather for a little over 5 years. After investing on my own for many years I started researching for a way to join a club in my town or online where I could invest real money alongside other teens. I searched all through my local area (Westchester County) as well as online for forums or virtual investment clubs. To my surprise, there were no organizations where a young investor like myself could invest his or her money alongside other likeminded teens. So I decided to create my organization, The Young Investors Club, LLC. I knew that to promote the club I would need a strong partner whose platform I could leverage to get initial interest. I first thought about my school, however based on what I'd observed I concluded there would be little chance the school would allow a club to be created which required money to join, especially since it would exclude those who could not afford the initial investment.

My next option was a business organization I had already created a smaller club with in the past. The organization had 20,000+ members as well as a very strong parent network and I knew they could be a very powerful ally if I were able to bring them on board. I brought the idea to the east coast family board representative. After 5 to 10 minutes of pitching he loved the idea and put me in touch with the right local people to pitch the idea further. After a month or two of getting through all the gatekeepers, I was finally informed I would need a club sponsor to help facilitate the club and get board approval. I contacted one member who seemed interested; however he decided to decline for personal reasons. Fortunately, I got the names of 4 more members of the larger business organization.

The first three all rejected me right off the bat; however the final response I got was "maybe," which after a call turned into a "yes." The member ran a financial advisory firm, which later ended up becoming very helpful in setting up our brokerage account, filing our taxes, and running the club's accounting. After 6 months of jumping through more hurdles, by the time March came around we finally launched the club. We sent out emails to about 150 New York families to run a beta test and see how much interest the club received. We received a few email responses and after many one-on-one parent phone calls I recruited our first 10 members into the club, each with an average check size of $750. Within our first year the club had risen to 21 members and $21,500 in assets under management (AUM).

By the time Junior year came around the club had steadily grown to 30-40 members. It was no doubt already a success. However, I decided this was going to be the year I dramatically expanded the club's membership and assets and turned it into the huge success I knew it could be. At that point, I had mainly grown the club through email blasts just to the local New York area, however to take the club to the next level I knew I would need to get new members from out of state. I requested several lists of all the chapter administrators' names and phone numbers for all the groups up and down the east coast. I began to go down the list and call and email every single one of them. There were over 30+ chapter admins I reached out to that month first by email pitches then by phone call pitches. Over the next 4-6 weeks I set up dozens of phone calls and sent out hundreds of emails (sometimes there were multiple people I needed to convince within one chapter). After tirelessly pushing though I had persuaded 75% of the North East Coast chapters to circulate news of the Young Investors Club to each of their local members.

As I quickly learned, the (marketing) component to running the club was one element, but the facilitation element was a whole different category. We had 5-10 new parents reaching out to us about membership EVERYDAY. Not to mention the back and forth emails, replying to follow up questions, hopping on phone calls to answer questions directly, accepting funds, etc. It was becoming too much for one person to handle.

I asked another member of the club to help participate in new member recruiting, applications, and record keeping. He graciously accepted and we set up an entire system which organized new members' applications, answered questions about how the club works, recorded the necessary information to accept funds, and kept track of all the deposits we received. Over two months, we had made over 100 phone calls, received and sent over 1000+ emails all while going to school every day, taking tests, doing homework, after school activities and all the other things a high school student has to do on a daily basis. By June of Junior year (8 months later) just as school was coming to an end, the club had grown from its initial membership of 20 members two years prior to close to 100 members and a portfolio worth over $115,000+. Today the club is one of the largest teen investment organizations in the world but perhaps more valuable than the size of the club is the number of teenagers we have been able to help educate on investing.

Many members of the club have gone on to start their own investment clubs in their local areas and have gained valuable insight in deciding how to make investments for their own portfolios. Through running the club I have become a teacher, mentor, and friend to many and it's been an honor to build and run.

CHAPTER TEN

MY THOUGHTS ON INVESTING IN FUNDS OR USING FINANCIAL ADVISORS

Recently I was pitched on investing my money with a financial advisor so I wanted to include a section about this that way you think twice before signing over your savings to an investment advisor.

Most of the time, over the long run, you are far better off simply investing your money in the S&P 500 (SPY for short) than investing your money in investment funds or with financial advisors. Financial advisors and investment funds charge fees (typically 1% or more of your total assets) and often their performance is worse than the long term annualized return of the S&P 500, which is around 9.8% per year.

"In 2008, Buffett bet the investment industry at large that a Vanguard index fund that invested in the S&P 500 would outperform any hedge fund over 10 years. Seides accepted the bet and put up a group of five hedge funds against the index fund. The bet doesn't officially end until December, but with the hedge funds averaging 2.2 percent returns since

2008, compared with more than 7 percent for the index fund, it's been clear for a while that Buffett has won. The prize is $1 million, donated to charity." - (Inc Magazine)

Buffet winning the bet makes a big statement. The old way of investing is coming to an end. Funds and advisors can no longer charge their huge fees for producing average returns and failing to beat the SPY year after year.

Time and time again you would have been better off investing your money in the SPY rather than trusting it with the so-called expert who think they can beat the market when they simply cannot. If you ever get a call from a financial advisor don't let them fool you, 9 times out of 10 you're better off investing your money in the S&P 500, 100% fee FREE.

CHAPTER ELEVEN

HOW TO TRACK YOUR INVESTMENTS/PORTFOLIO MONITORING?

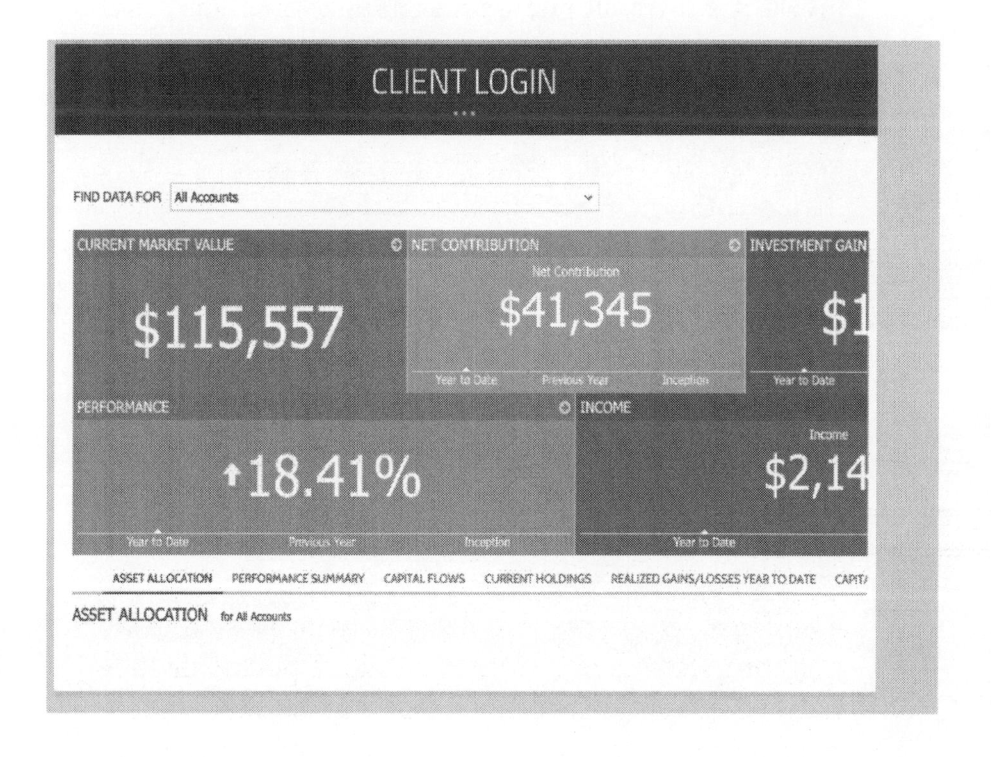

Before you begin investing, if you are under the age of 18, you'll want to find a parent or guardian who can open a custodial brokerage account for you. You can use any brokerage firm to open the account;

however, the top 4 largest ones are Fidelity, Charles Shwawb, E*TRADE, and TD Ameritrade (I personally use fidelity).

Next, you'll want to decide how much money you want to put in your investment account. I would recommend putting 100% of your savings into the investment account (you don't necessarily need to invest it all) it will just be available in case you want to make a quick trade. Of the money you have in the account I would recommend investing 70-80% of your cash because of your minimal day to day expenses as a teenager. One important tip is the time you decide to open an investment account might not be the same time you'll want to make your first investment. I would recommend following the market for a month or two before you make your first investment that way you start to learn market behavior and you can decide on your own whether you're buying into your investments at a good price.

Remember sometimes the price you pay can be more important than the past performance of the company. After you've bought all your positions it's now time to manage your portfolio. I personally like to check on my investment accounts each once a month just to see where we're at. However, for a passive investor whose making investments in companies for the long run it's not necessary to re-evaluate or change your portfolio for months or even years. The stock market is meant to be a long term game, not a short term one. If you believe a company is a good investment long term, the stock price a month or two months later should not affect your opinion of value of that company over the long run.

FINAL NOTES

Wealth building is an essential skill throughout one's life. It can single-handedly determine what kind of quality of life you live as well as how long you have to work. I truly hope you've got a lot out of this book in terms of how to approach teen investing and how to analyze investments. As a teenager myself I know how crucial investing can be and how meaningful an impact it can make on your life. I leave you with this one final note. If you had found a way to work and save on a consistent basis and by the time you were 18 years old you built up a portfolio worth $10,000 from summer jobs and other side hustles and you added an additional $5,000 per year you earn from a job in your early 20s and you invested it in the S&P 500 index, which as I pointed out earlier takes little to no effort, earning an average of 9.8% return per year by the time you were 38 years old not even having reached 40 you would have a total portfolio value of $362,000. That's enough to pay for an entire house!

So I encourage you to continue to work and invest your money and I promise one day in the future you will be so thankful you did. I want to say a special thanks to my grandfather who helped me write this book and who has taught me so much about the markets and investing over the last 10 years.

Lastly, if you're interested in learning more about investing, check out my virtual course. It's normally $297 but for readers of this book it's only $79. Here's the link to get the course >> https://bit.ly/TeenInvestingCourse

I go over my own investing techniques, walk you through how I built my portfolio, and give you review sheets on best investing practices.

Other than that, I wish you great success on your lifelong investing journey!

If you found this book helpful, please consider leaving a review on Amazon so more readers can enjoy it!

P.S. Let me know about any success stories…

If you're ever looking for advice reach out to me at jackrose1824@gmail.com (Don't be afraid to email me I get tons of emails and reply to all of them within 24 hours)

Disclaimer

Do your Own Research

Our content is intended to be used and must be used for informational purposes only. It is very important to do your own analysis before making any investment based on your own personal circumstances. You should take independent financial advice from a professional in connection with, or independently research and verify, any information that you find in this book and wish to rely upon, whether for the purpose of making an investment decision or otherwise.

The content is for informational purposes only, you should not construe any such information or other material as legal, tax, investment, financial, or other advice. Nothing contained in this book constitutes a solicitation, recommendation, endorsement, or offer by the author to buy or sell any securities or other financial instruments in this or in in any other jurisdiction in which such solicitation or offer would be unlawful under the securities laws of such jurisdiction.

All content in this book is information of a general nature and does not address the circumstances of any particular individual or entity. Nothing in this book constitutes professional and/or financial advice, nor does any information in this book constitute a comprehensive or complete statement of the matters discussed or the law relating thereto. The author is not a fiduciary by virtue of any person's use of or access to this book.

You alone assume the sole responsibility of evaluating the merits and risks associated with the use of any information or other content in this book before making any decisions based on such information or other content.

REFERENCES

Harvey, C. R. (2012). *Stock*. Retrieved from The Free Dictionary by Farlex: https://financial-dictionary.thefreedictionary.com/stock

Marketwatch Virtual Stock Exchange. (n.d.). Retrieved from MarketWatch: https://www.marketwatch.com/game

Picardo, E. (2019, June 25). *Investing*. Retrieved from Investopedia: https://www.investopedia.com/terms/i/investing.asp

Stock. (2019, December 5). Retrieved from Financial Glossary: https://financial-dictionary.thefreedictionary.com/stock

Wall Street Words: An A to Z Guide to Investment Terms for Today's Investor. (2009). Retrieved from Farlex Financial Dictionary: https://financial-dictionary.thefreedictionary.com/stock

Zetlin, M. (n.d.). *Here's What That Can Teach You About Making Decisions*. Retrieved from Inc.: https://www.inc.com/minda-zetlin/warren-buffet-won-a-1-million-bet-heres-what-that.html

Made in the USA
Monee, IL
26 November 2021